Birds in
PARADISE

Rob Warin

D0584522

HEINLE
CENGAGE Learning

Australia • Brazil • Japan • Korea • Mexico • Singapore • Spain • United Kingdom • United States

Words to Know

This story happens in the Caribbean [kærɪbiən] country of Trinidad and Tobago [trɪnɪdæd and təbeɪgoʊ]. It happens on the island of Trinidad.

A **Trinidad's Birds.** Read the definitions. Then label the items in the picture with the underlined words.

A beak is the hard, pointed part of a bird's mouth.
Wings are the flat parts of the body which a bird uses for flying.
A nest is a home built by animals, especially birds.
A hummingbird is a very small, brightly colored bird which moves very quickly.

1. _____

2. _____

3. _____

B The Island of Trinidad. Read the paragraph. Then use the underlined words to complete the sentences.

Trinidad is a tropical island that is famous for its birds and other wildlife. The topography of the area consists of mostly forests and mountains. The atmosphere, or feeling of the island, is very pleasant. It's so beautiful that some people think it's like paradise. One man, Roger Neckles [rɒdʒər nɛkəlz], has made it his life's work to study the beautiful birds of Trinidad. He's an ornithologist.

1. Animals and plants that live in natural conditions are called _____.

2. An _____ is a person who studies birds.

3. The _____ is the general feel of an area.

4. _____ is a perfect place that is often considered to be imaginary or hard to find.

5. A _____ is a piece of land with water around it that is in a very hot part of the world.

6. The shape and characteristics of the land in an area is the _____.

4. _____

It's very early in the morning on the tropical island of Trinidad. Colorful tropical birds are flying everywhere and moving around in the trees. They're calling to one another and you can see their beautiful colors among all the different greens of the island. However, they're not the only ones who are awake on this early morning. Ornithologist and photographer Roger Neckles is up and moving too.

🎧 CD 1, Track 01

For the past ten years, Neckles has been living on the island and taking photographs of the island's birds. As he walks along, he makes a sound like a hummingbird. He wants to attract the birds with this 'bird call'—and he does! A hummingbird flies so close by that Neckles can hear it! "We just got **buzzed**[1] by a hummingbird," he says excitedly. "Did you hear that?"

As he continues walking around the island, Neckles talks about the beauty around him. It's clear that he really loves the place. He describes it as being like **heaven**.[2] He talks about how incredibly beautiful Trinidad is with its many colorful flowers and birds flying everywhere. Because of this, Neckles feels it's just like paradise. So what does he do every day in this 'bird paradise'?

---

[1] **buzz:** pass by very quickly
[2] **heaven:** a lovely place where good people go when they die according to some religions

Neckles talks about his day as he drives into the mountains. "This is the best time of the day for me," he says, "getting up at five o'clock in the morning… **heading off into the sticks**[3] up in the mountains." As he continues, he describes the area itself, "The atmosphere…the temperature up here…it's just fantastic! You **breathe pure oxygen**!"[4] He then adds happily, "This is a typical 'day in the office' for me."

---

[3]**head off into the sticks:** go into an area which is a long way from a town or city

[4]**breathe pure oxygen:** take very clean air into the body

a Purple Honeycreeper

Neckles works at the Asa Wright Nature Center, which attracts ornithologists and bird lovers from all over the world. People go there especially to view some of the world's most attractive and special birds. However, this isn't easy since the birds move very quickly! Neckles explains that he has to be very fast when he shoots photos, or he'll miss his opportunity. Just as he says this, a beautiful purple bird with black on its wings appears. "Look at that Purple Honeycreeper!" he points out. "Whoa! The color is so **unique**,[5] [it's] a fantastic shade of purple," he adds as he takes a few photos.

There are about 460 different types of birds on the island. Neckles is trying to photograph them all, but it takes time. He has to wait for just the right moment. According to Neckles, "If you are not prepared to wait for the [right photographic] shot, you won't get it."

---

[5]**unique:** unusual in a good way

Neckles has studied hummingbird behavior and bird calls for a long time. He also knows most things about their way of life, including where they live. Hummingbirds live in very unusual nests that they build using their beaks and feet. Neckles comments that the birds are very skillful in the way they make their nests. He explains: "They're really strong, they build them on the very edges of branches, and winds come—**hurricanes**[6] will come, and **gale force winds**[7]—and they won't **blow down**."[8]

---

[6]**hurricane:** a storm with a very strong wind
[7]**gale force wind:** a very strong wind that is nearly as strong as a hurricane
[8]**blow down:** fall down due to wind

Scan for Information

Scan pages 11 and 12 to find the information. Circle the correct answer.

1. Neckles works at (home/a nature center/ a school).

2. There are (150/380/460) different types of birds in Trinidad.

3. Hummingbird nests are very (strong/ weak/windy).

a butterfly

a bird

14

Why has Neckles chosen to study birds in Trinidad and Tobago? He explains: "I came here in 1978, and I was so **enchanted with**[9] the topography of the land here in Trinidad and Tobago that I thought, 'Oh yes! I could do this.'"

Through his research, Neckles has developed a deeper understanding not only of the birds, but of all the wildlife of the island—even the ones that are not so pretty. "Whoa, you don't want to get your fingers in there," he says as he touches the dangerous-looking mouth of a large, black insect.

---

[9]**(be) enchanted with:** like very much

an insect

There are many kinds of wildlife in Trinidad and Tobago, including insects, birds, and butterflies.

However, it's not just any wildlife that brings Neckles into the woods again and again. It's the birds. This morning he hopes to get a photograph of a very small—and very rare—bird. It's a bird that people hardly ever get a chance to see. Then Neckles suddenly exclaims, "Look at this!" He's found, or 'spotted', the bird!

"This is the most **festive**[10] hummingbird in Trinidad and Tobago!" he explains as he prepares to photograph the bird. "[It's] the smallest hummingbird in Trinidad and Tobago—the **Tufted Coquette**.[11] Look at him just sitting there," Neckles says as he moves in to get his photo. He's been trying to photograph this hummingbird for six weeks. It's been a very long wait, and now it comes down to one chance …

---

[10]**festive:** very colorful and enjoyable to see
[11]**Tufted Coquette:** [tʌftɪd koʊkɛt]

… and he gets it! Neckles has finally gotten the photo that he has been seeking for six weeks! "Yes! I got it!" he exclaims. Neckles is very excited. "I've got **goosebumps**[12] all up my arms. This is fantastic!" he says.

In the end, Neckles doesn't mind waiting for the perfect moment to take a photograph. Like the birds he follows, he enjoys the day and the beauty around him. And as for Neckles' future? "I have no plans to give this up at all because I figure I could do this for the rest of my life," he says. "Every time I go out, I see something new," he explains. Apparently, the birds of Trinidad aren't the only ones who have found paradise!

---

[12] **goosebumps:** small, raised parts on the skin that appear because of cold, fear, or excitement

What do you think?

1. What are some of the good and bad points about Neckles' job?

2. Would you like to do a job like this? Why or why not?

3. What kinds of wildlife do you like? What kinds don't you like?

After You Read

1. On page 4, the word 'calling' means the birds are:
   A. moving their wings
   B. making sounds
   C. looking for food
   D. flying from tree to tree

2. A good heading for paragraph 1 on page 7 is:
   A. Tropical Paradise for Neckles
   B. Hummingbird Flies Away
   C. Ornithologist Attracts Bird
   D. Neckles Loves Tropical Island

3. In paragraph 2 on page 7,'it' in 'he describes it' refers to:
   A. the island
   B. beauty
   C. a bird
   D. heaven

4. What part of his job does Neckles NOT like?
   A. the air
   B. waking up early
   C. the drive
   D. none of the above

5. Why does Neckles have to be fast when taking photos?
   A. because birds move suddenly
   B. because birds hide from cameras
   C. because the colors are fantastic
   D. because birds are noisy

6. What view is expressed by Neckles in paragraph 2 on page 11?
   A. Trinidad has too many birds.
   B. Taking photos of the birds is easy.
   C. Good bird photography takes time.
   D. Hummingbirds are unique.

7. Neckles really likes the topography _____ the islands.
   A. of
   B. in
   C. from
   D. at

8. In paragraph 2 on page 15, 'ones' refers to:
   A. birds
   B. islands
   C. fingers
   D. animals

9. In paragraph 1 on page 16, the word 'rare' means that the bird is:
   A. unpopular
   B. uncommon
   C. common
   D. popular

10. Which is a good heading for paragraph 1 on page 18?
   A. Missed Chance
   B. Long Wait Is Over
   C. Six Weeks More
   D. Biggest Bird Found

11. Why does Neckles get goosebumps?
   A. He is cold from waiting.
   B. He is nervous near the bird.
   C. He is happy he got the shot.
   D. His arms are tired.

12. What's the main idea of paragraph 2 on page 18?
   A. Neckles makes plans to leave the island.
   B. Neckles takes photographs too slowly.
   C. Neckles wants to change his life.
   D. Neckles wants to stay in Trinidad.

Missing Bird *Spotted*

An Ivory-Billed Woodpecker

In the past, there were thousands of ivory-billed woodpeckers in the United States, especially in the states of Florida, Texas, and Arkansas. Until recently, ornithologists believed that these birds had died out. No one had seen an ivory-billed woodpecker in the United States for over sixty years. However, on May 21, 2005, several members of a research team were traveling down the Choctawhatchee River in Florida. There, they thought they saw an ivory-billed woodpecker. Later, they heard the unusual sound these woodpeckers make when they strike their beak on the surface of a tree. The research team reportedly had goosebumps as they began to hope that the ivory-billed woodpecker hadn't died out after all.

Soon a search team was organized. They returned to the river and began recording the sounds of the wildlife in the area. The team carried small cassette

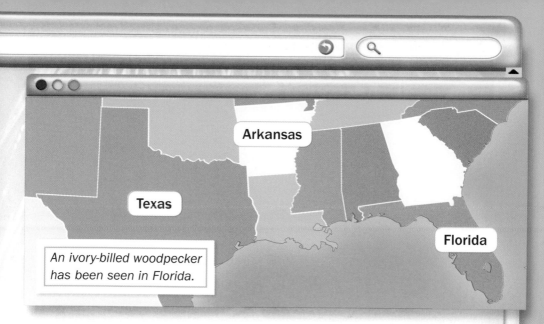

Arkansas

Texas

Florida

An ivory-billed woodpecker has been seen in Florida.

recorders and set up other listening stations near the river. They then sent recordings of some of these bird sounds to the University of Windsor in Canada. The university students carefully compared the new recordings with old recordings of ivory-billed woodpeckers. The new recordings indicated that there are probably at least two ivory-billed woodpeckers living near the Choctawhatchee River. With this news comes the hope that where there are two, there may be many more. If this discovery has encouraged you to search for an ivory-billed woodpecker in your area, read our guide below:

HOW TO SPOT AN IVORY-BILLED WOODPECKER

The ivory-billed woodpecker is a large bird. It has a distinctive light yellow beak and unusual white edges on both the tops and bottoms of its wings. It also has thin, white lines that run down its neck and back. This special woodpecker lives in areas where there are a lot of trees and very few people. These birds are still very rare, so please report any possible sightings to your local bird-watching group.

CD 1, Track 02

Word Count: 332
Time: _____

Vocabulary List

atmosphere (3, 8)

beak (2, 12)

blow down (12)

breathe pure oxygen (8)

buzz (7)

enchanted with (15)

festive (16)

gale force wind (12)

goosebumps (18)

head off into the sticks (8)

heaven (7, 18)

hummingbird (2, 7, 12, 13, 16)

hurricane (12)

nest (2, 12, 13)

ornithologist (3, 4, 11)

paradise (3, 7, 18)

topography (3, 15)

tropical island (3, 4)

unique (11)

wildlife (3, 15, 16)

wing (2, 11)